ALEJANDRO

Words and Music by STEFANI GERMANOTTA
and NADIR KHAYAT

Moderate Pop feel

To Coda

BAD ROMANCE

Words and Music by STEFANI GERMANOTTA
and NADIR KHAYAT

Moderate Techno groove

BORN THIS WAY

Words and Music by STEFANI GERMANOTTA,
JEPPE LAURSEN, PAUL BLAIR
and FERNANDO GARIBAY

Energetic Pop

THE FAME

Words and Music by STEFANI GERMANOTTA
and MARTIN KIERSZENBAUM

Moderate Dance groove

18

THE EDGE OF GLORY

Words and Music by STEFANI GERMANOTTA,
PAUL BLAIR and FERNANDO GARIBAY

24

JUST DANCE

Words and Music by STEFANI GERMANOTTA,
REDONE and ALIAUNE THIAM

TELEPHONE

Words and Music by BEYONCE KNOWLES,
LASHAWN DANIELS, LAZONATE FRANKLIN,
RODNEY JERKINS and STEFANI GERMANOTTA

To Coda ⊕

LOVEGAME

Words and Music by STEFANI GERMANOTTA
and REDONE

Moderate Dance groove

To Coda

PAPARAZZI

Words and Music by STEFANI GERMANOTT
and ROB FUSA

Moderate Techno groove

42

POKER FACE

Words and Music by STEFANI GERMANOTT
and REDON

Dance Pop

STARSTRUCK

Words and Music by STEFANI GERMANOTTA,
TRAMAR DILLARD, MARTIN KIERSZENBAUM
and NICK DRESTI

Moderate groove

50

YOÜ AND I

Words and Music by
STEFANI GERMANOTT

Power Ballad

D.S. al Cod

CODA